*For John and Viv Burton, who have spent
a lifetime preserving the pattern
N. D.*

*For Mark and Feste
E. S.*

CANDLEWICK PRESS

• First U.S. edition 2017 • Library of Congress Catalog Card Number pending • ISBN 978-0-7636-9483-8 • This book has been typeset in Gill Sans MT • The illustrations were done in watercolor • Candlewick Press, 99 Dover Street, Somerville, Massachusetts 02144 • visit us at www.candlewick.com • Printed in Shenzhen, Guangdong, China • 17 18 19 20 21 22 CCP 10 9 8 7 6 5 4 3 2 1

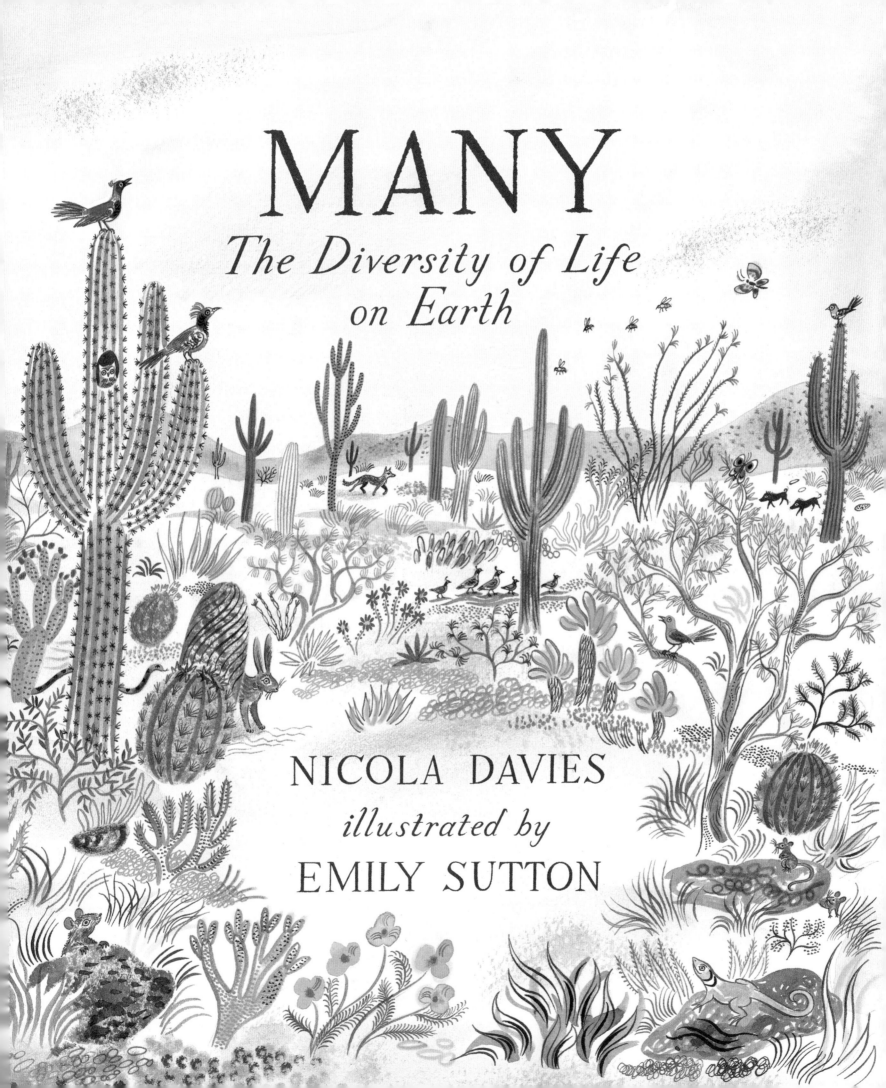

# MANY

## *The Diversity of Life on Earth*

### NICOLA DAVIES

*illustrated by*

### EMILY SUTTON

How many different **kinds** of living things
are there on our planet?

One,

two,

three,

MANY!

Yes! There are SO MANY!

From big things, like elephants
and oak trees . . .

*There are two kinds*
*of elephants, African and Asian,*
*and more than six hundred kinds of oak trees.*

to small things, like mushrooms . . .

*So far, scientists have counted*
*one hundred thousand kinds of mushrooms.*

and microbes.

*Microbes are so small, you need a microscope to see them.*
*There can be five thousand kinds in just one teaspoon of dirt!*

Everywhere you look, there are living things.

In deserts . . .

on islands far out at sea . . .

FEATHER MITES

under the feathers of birds
and on the backs of beetles . . .

*Lichen beetles have
tiny plants growing on their backs,
which help them to stay hidden and safe.*

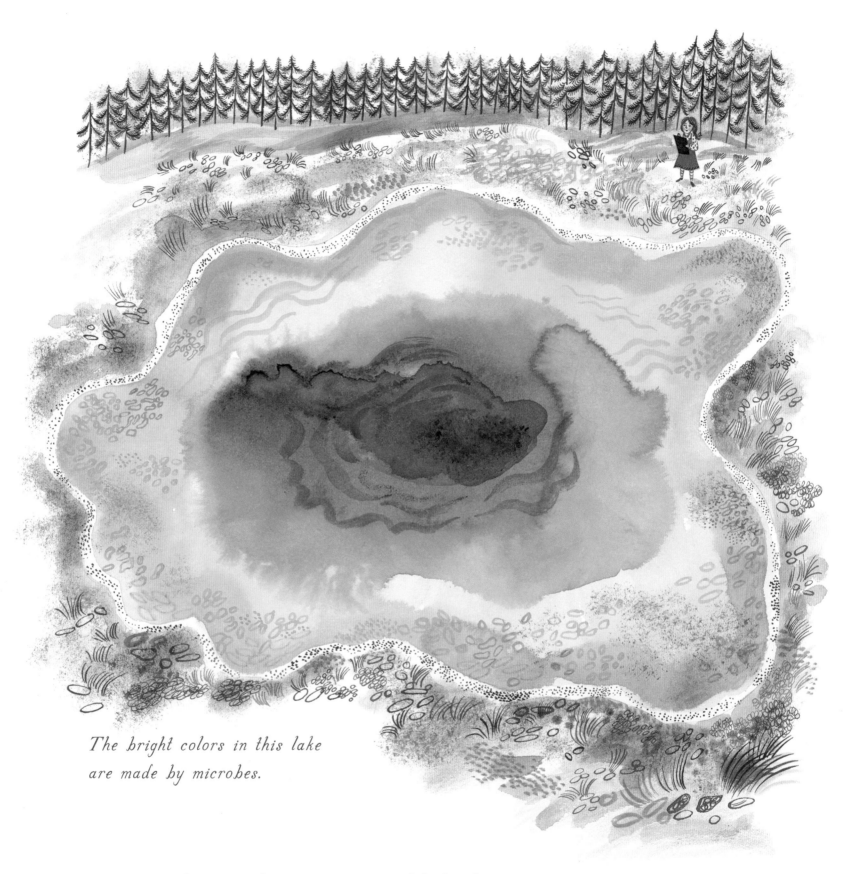

*The bright colors in this lake
are made by microbes.*

even in places where you would think
nothing at all could live, like boiling volcanic lakes.

Counting **how many** kinds there are can be difficult,
because some places are hard to look in . . .

like the tops of tall trees in the jungle . . .

or the
bottom of the
coldest seas.

It can also be difficult because, sometimes, things that look different are really the same . . .

YOUNG QUEEN ANGELFISH

ADULT QUEEN ANGELFISH

and things that look the same are really different.

VICEROY
BUTTERFLY

MONARCH
BUTTERFLY

But mainly it's difficult because there are just *so many* living things!

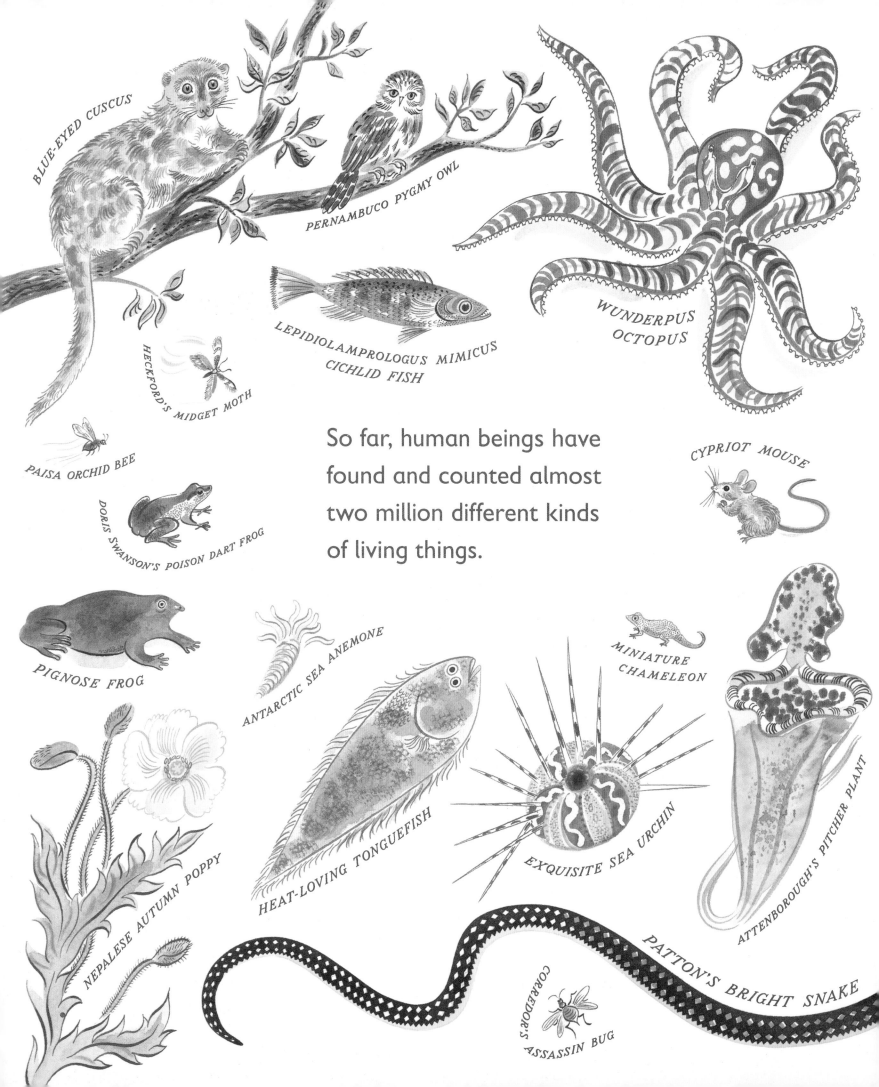

BLUE-EYED CUSCUS

PERNAMBUCO PYGMY OWL

WUNDERPUS OCTOPUS

HECKFORD'S MIDGET MOTH

LEPIDIOLAMPROLOGUS MIMICUS CICHLID FISH

PAISA ORCHID BEE

CYPRIOT MOUSE

DORIS SWANSON'S POISON DART FROG

So far, human beings have found and counted almost two million different kinds of living things.

PIGNOSE FROG

ANTARCTIC SEA ANEMONE

MINIATURE CHAMELEON

NEPALESE AUTUMN POPPY

HEAT-LOVING TONGUEFISH

EXQUISITE SEA URCHIN

ATTENBOROUGH'S PITCHER PLANT

CORREDOR'S ASSASSIN BUG

PATTON'S BRIGHT SNAKE

SWALLOWTAIL APPALACHIAN TIGER

GALÁPAGOS ROSY IGUANA

DIAMANTINA TARANTULA

ANDRE MENEZ'S CONE SNAIL

SHOCKING PINK DRAGON MILLIPEDE

CRYPTIC FOREST FALCON

But that's only the start. There could be many millions more. Thousands of new species are found every year.

SIAU ISLAND TARSIER

BARBIE PAGODA FUNGUS

GREY-FACED SENGI

SPONGEBOB FUNGUS

CHILD OF CYPRIS TINY FISH

BONAIRE BANDED BOX JELLY

GOLDEN V KELP

*All the living things on this page have been found in the last fifty years.*

TENNESSEE BOTTLEBRUSH CRAYFISH

And the more we find, the more we learn about how living things depend on one another—for food, for places to live, and for ways to grow.

*Jaguars eat pacas, which eat the fruits and seeds from trees.*

*Hummingbirds eat insects and nectar, and insects eat nectar.*

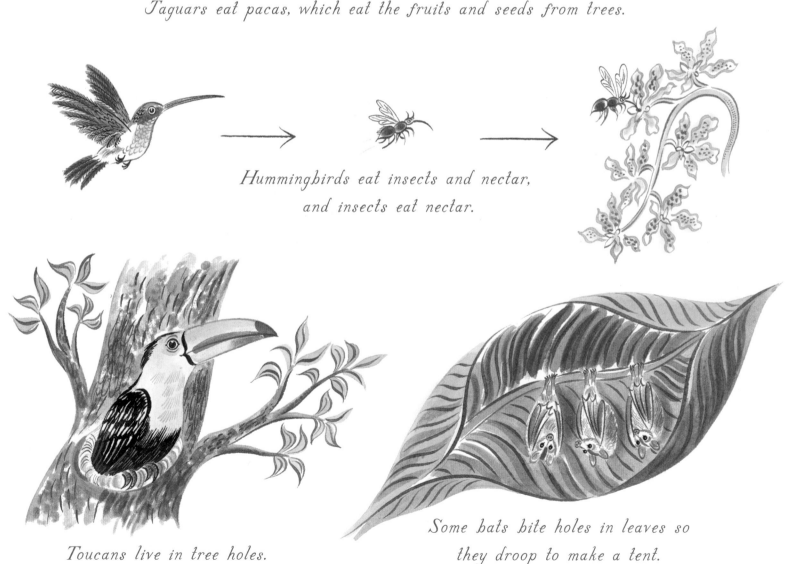

*Toucans live in tree holes.*

*Some bats bite holes in leaves so they droop to make a tent.*

Pacas poop out the tree seeds they've eaten, which grow into new trees.

Baby frogs grow in pools of rainwater in leaves.

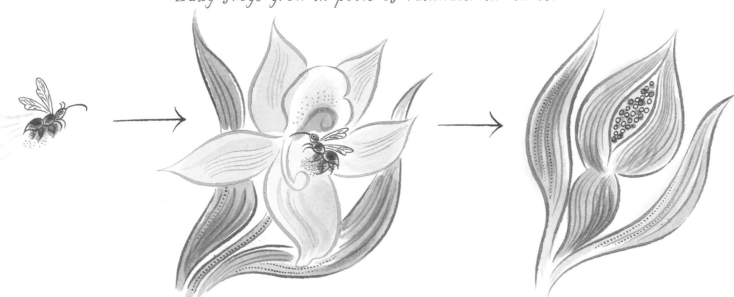

Bees carry pollen to flowers, which allows flowers to grow seeds.

We have learned that every
kind of living thing is part of a big,
beautiful, complicated pattern.

The trouble is, all over the world, human beings
are destroying pieces of the pattern . . .

*Chemicals poison the air, rivers, and oceans.*

*Fishing boats take too much from the sea.*

*People build roads that divide forests into pieces.*

causing animals
and plants to disappear.

# EXTINCT

MAUKE STARLING

MADEIRAN LARGE WHITE

CAROLINA PARAKEET

ZANZIBAR LEOPARD

PYRENEAN IBEX

RÉUNION GIANT TORTOISE

DODO

TASMANIAN WOLF

Many kinds of living things have already been lost.

# SPECIES

DELCOURT'S GIANT GECKO

BUSH WREN

MASCARENE PARROT

NORFOLK KAKA

PASSENGER PIGEON

GOLDEN TOAD

LAUGHING OWL

MAURITIUS BLUE PIGEON

MARTINIQUE CURLY-TAILED LIZARD

CHOISEUL PIGEON

EASTERN HARE-WALLABY

GOULD'S MOUSE

VIETNAMESE JAVAN RHINOCEROS

Some have disappeared before we've had a chance to find them.

Human beings are part of
the pattern, too, and we need to
make sure it stays big, beautiful,
and complicated . . .

because we could
not keep living on Earth
if we had to count down
instead of up . . .

from MANY

to one.